Sew
Eco-Friendly

First published in 2021

Search Press Limited
Wellwood, North Farm Road,
Tunbridge Wells, Kent TN2 3DR

Photographs by Garie Hind

ISBN: 978-1-78221-926-2
ebook ISBN: 978-1-78126-920-6

The projects in this book have been made using
metric measurements, and the imperial equivalents
provided have been calculated following standard
conversion practices. Always use either imperial or
metric measurements, not a combination of both.

Suppliers
For details of suppliers, please visit
the Search Press website:
www.searchpress.com

For further inspiration, visit Debbie's website:
www.debbieshoresewing.com
Or join the Half Yard™ Sewing Club:
www.halfyardsewingclub.com

Sew
Eco-Friendly

25 reusable projects for sustainable sewing

Debbie Shore

SEARCH PRESS

Contents

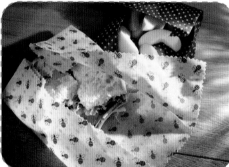

Make-up Remover Pads,
page 18

Wax Sandwich Wrap,
page 20

Wax Snack Pouch,
page 22

Bath Sponges,
page 24

Hemp Tote Bag,
page 26

Baby Wipe Bag,
page 30

Bottle Bag,
page 38

Stocking Gift Bags,
page 40

Grocery Bag,
page 44

Plant Pot Covers,
page 48

Fabric Gift Wrap,
page 50

Gift Cube,
page 54

Gift Bags,
page 58

Repair Kit,
page 62

Bowl Covers,
page 68

Apron,
page 70

Wipes: Baby wipes, Tumble
drier sheets, Kitchen wipes,
page 74

Foldaway Bag,
page 76

Cork Lunchbag,
page 80

Cutlery Roll,
page 84

Face Coverings: Simple mask,
Shaped mask, Mask carry
pouch, page 88

Introduction

Trying to reduce wastage is something we're all conscious of, so I've put together projects in this book that can either replace single-use items, such as wipes and cotton wool pads, or create items that can be used over again, like the gift packaging and bags. I've tried to use organic fabrics where possible but of course these can be costly, so upcycling is an ideal and affordable option. When you visit a charity shop/thrift store, focus on the fabrics in front of you, rather than the garments they're made into!

Always remember that small changes can make a big difference, so be proud of yourself for the small steps you're taking.

Debbie
x

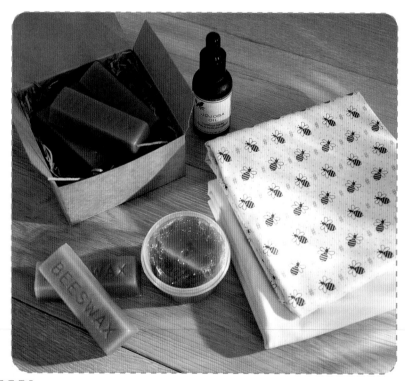

10 tips for the complete beginner

1 Start with a simple project such as the wipes (see page 74) – there's nothing easier than hemming squares! This can even be done by hand.

2 To help you sew in a straight line and create even seam allowances, place a strip of masking tape over the bed of your sewing machine as a guide for your fabric (an elastic band around the free arm works well too). Measure from the needle 5mm (¼in) to the right and place your tape at this point. Throughout the book, seam allowances are 5mm (¼in) unless otherwise stated.

3 Topstitching – a visible line of stitching – can be a bit daunting, so sew slowly. If you're not very confident, use a thread that matches your fabric so that it doesn't stand out too much. If you have a presser foot with a guide, such as a blind hem foot, use the guide around the edge of the fabric to help keep your stitches straight.

4 Don't be afraid of trying a new type of fabric or a different technique... we all sewed our first zip, we all cut our first bias binding strips and we all used (and still use!) our stitch unpickers!

5 You don't need the most expensive sewing machine. If you're just starting out, try to borrow one... after all, you may not wish to continue!

6 Reverse a couple of stitches at the start and end of your sewing line. Some machines have a 'fix' or 'lock' stitch that puts three or four tiny stitches close together. This will stop the stitches coming undone.

7 Change your sewing-machine needle regularly. It is recommended you put a new needle in after every eight hours of sewing – you'll notice a difference to the stitches and even the sound of your machine! It's always good form when you change the needle to take off the needle plate and clean out any lint. (Take a look at your manufacturer's instructions.)

8 There are a few projects in this book that involve sewing curves, so take them slowly. If you need to pivot the fabric, stop with your needle in the down position to keep the stitch line smooth.

9 Add a personal touch. You don't need to stick to my designs exactly – try changing the shape of the flap on the baby wipe bag (page 30), use different embroidery techniques on the hemp tote (page 26) and embellish the gift cubes (page 54) with lace or appliqué to make the projects your own!

10 Don't worry if things go a bit wrong – put your work down and come back to it the next day. It won't seem half as bad as you first thought!

Materials & tools

Fabrics

Wherever possible in this book I've used sustainable or recycled fabrics. These may prove to be quite expensive, but remember you're making products that will last for many years to come!

CORK FABRIC

This is a fabric backed with strips of cork, which is predominantly grown in Portugal. Removing the cork bark from the trees doesn't harm them and it can be harvested every nine to ten years. It is amazingly easy to work with: it's soft and pliable, crease-resistant, wipe-clean, antibacterial and its seams don't need to be finished. A walking or non-stick presser foot will help when sewing, and try to use fabric clips instead of pins so as not to leave holes in the fabric. This is a perfect fabric for bag making and looks stylish when mixed with contrasting textures such as hemp.

HEMP

Hemp fabric is plant-based – the outer layer of the plant has rope-like fibres and it is very fast growing. It is a strong, durable, antibacterial and long-lasting fabric, is easily dyed, and becomes softer after each wash.

RECYCLED COTTON

Fibres are collected together by colour so no dyeing is needed, they are sorted and graded then reused to make new fabrics (synthetic fibres can also be recycled). Weights of fabric can vary – I used a canvas weight for my bottle bag (see page 38).

LINEN

From flax to fabric: linen is one of the oldest fabrics in history, and is made from the cellulose fibres that grow inside the stalks of the flax plant. It is breathable, absorbent and is a favoured fabric for clothing in hot climates. The downside is its creasing, but this reduces over time with washing.

RECYCLED POLYESTER

Plastic bottles are cut, chopped, melted and made into flakes, which then produce polyester fabric. The appearance of the fabric can range from the denim-like fabric I used for my grocery bag (see page 44) to soft furnishing fabrics.

COTTON

Cotton is the most popular fabric in the world due to its easy care, versatility, and breathability. It comes in many different weights from fine cotton lawn through to heavy canvas. Organic cotton is created using no pesticides and in certified factories; only natural dyes are used.

BAMBOO

The bamboo plant's fast growth rate and its ability to grow in a range of different climates with no need for pesticides make this an increasingly popular fabric. Knits, towelling, wadding/batting and weaves can be used for anything from bedding to clothing. The fabrics have a silky, smooth texture and are easy to care for. I've used bamboo towelling for my wipes (see page 74).

HESSIAN/BURLAP

Hessian/burlap is a coarse fabric made from the skin of the jute plant, sometimes mixed with other plants. More refined fabric is sometimes just called 'jute'. This strong fabric is good for bag making.

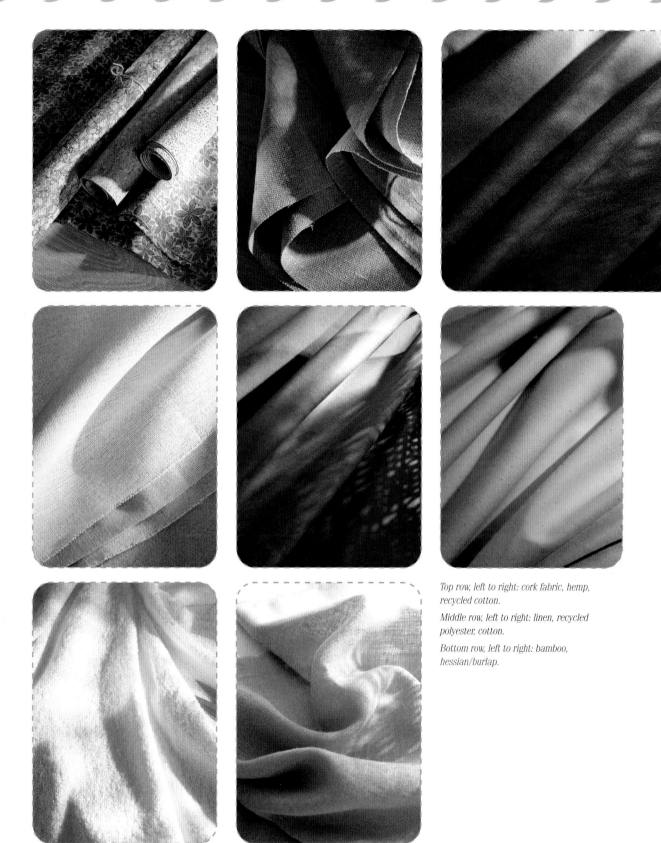

Top row, left to right: cork fabric, hemp, recycled cotton.

Middle row, left to right: linen, recycled polyester, cotton.

Bottom row, left to right: bamboo, hessian/burlap.

Threads

Although cotton thread is made from natural fibres, it may be more eco-friendly to use recycled polyester thread, made from plastic bottles. Polyester thread is strong, making it the perfect thread for grocery bags, and works with any type of fabric.

Wadding/batting

This is the layer of padding put between two pieces of fabric to give structure, warmth and a luxurious feel to a project. It can be made from many different fibres: cotton, polyester, silk, wool or bamboo, to name a few, and sometimes several fibres mixed together. The big decision is choosing a type. A lot depends on what you're using it for, and whether the item will be washed. I like natural, organic, untreated fibres for breathability and softness, and prefer types that are fire retardant.

The 'loft' refers to the thickness of the wadding/batting: the higher the loft the thicker the wadding/batting. Low loft is preferred for quilting.

Fusible fleece gives structure and is simply ironed onto the wrong side of your fabric – some types contain thermal threads, making them perfect for insulation or heat protection.

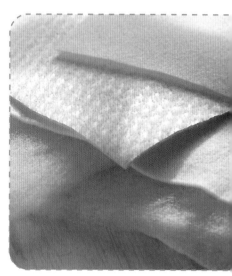

Sewing machine

I always recommend a computerized machine. They're simple to use, and have a comprehensive range of stitches that are automatically set to the required stitch width, length and tension. Make sure your machine comes with a guarantee and support. The projects in this book can be made with quite a basic machine, so don't think you have to spend a lot of money on one.

Cutting your fabric

ROTARY CUTTER, RULER AND MAT

Well worth the investment, these tools will help you measure and cut accurately and quickly. The most-used size of rotary cutter is 45mm (1¾in); use with a long acrylic ruler and a self-healing cutting mat (the bigger the better!) to ensure the most accurate straight-line cutting.

SHEARS

Shears aren't just for dressmaking; they have angled blades to help keep your fabric flat and ensure accurate cutting on larger items and thicker layers of fabric.

PINKING SHEARS

For finishing seams or cutting curves, pinking shears are a useful tool to have in your sewing box. They can also add a decorative edge on non-woven fabrics such as felt!

Securing your fabric

Use quality pins with large heads – this will ensure that the pins are easy to remove as you sew... and easy to spot if you drop them! For thicker fabrics or multiple layers you may need to use fabric clips, rather than pins.

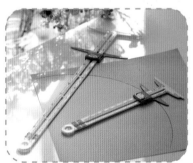

Marking your fabric

There are lots of options available to you. Air-erasable pens deliver ink that disappears after a few hours, while water-erasable ink washes away. I tend to use heat-erasable ink pens in the seam allowance – the ink will disappear using either friction or heat from the iron. Fabric pencils are useful and are available in both light and dark colours so they stand out against any fabric. Chalk is an option, but I find it can be difficult to make an accurate mark with chalk.

SLIDING GAUGES

These tools will help to measure and mark seams and hems, and can also be used to mark curves and circles on your fabric.

Bodkins

Safety pins are fine to help thread elastic and ribbon through channels, but you might want to invest in a bodkin to make threading quick and simple!

Useful stitches

Machine stitches

STRAIGHT STITCH

This straight, single line stitch is the most commonly used on any project. Lengthen the stitch to create a tacking/basting or gathering stitch; shorten the length to make the seam stronger. A triple straight stitch creates a dense line that is effective for topstitching, as well as being a useful stitch for stretch fabrics.

ZIGZAG STITCH

Not just a decorative stitch, a zigzag stitch can help to stop fabric from fraying so can be used to finish seams. Try altering the length and width of the stitches for different effects. One of the uses is for appliqué, where a dense line, known as satin stitch, is used to sew around fabric shapes.

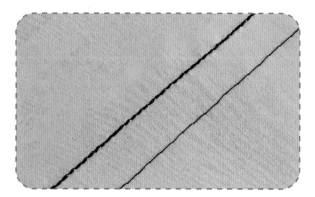

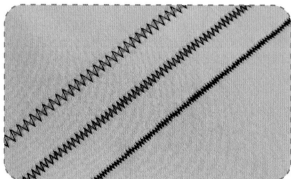

Hand stitches

SLIP STITCH

I use this to finish off bias binding and for hems. Keep the stitch to a short length and try to catch just a couple of strands of the fold of the bias binding to keep the stitch as small and invisible as possible. (See bias binding on pages 16–17.)

LADDER STITCH

This is the perfect stitch for closing turning gaps or making repairs in seams. Take the needle from one side of the opening to the opposite side, then gently pull to close the gap. Small stitches are the least visible.

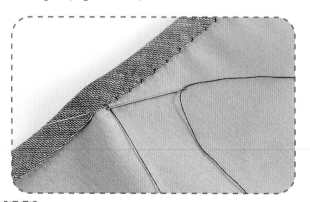

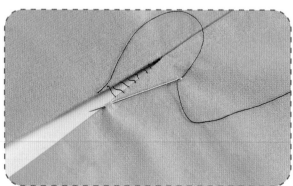

FRENCH KNOT

I used this stitch to create the poppies on my hemp tote bag (see page 26), and it's one of the most popular embroidery stitches for the centres of flowers. For my poppies, I took three strands of embroidery thread/floss and wrapped the thread around the needle four or five times. The more times you wrap, the larger the knot.

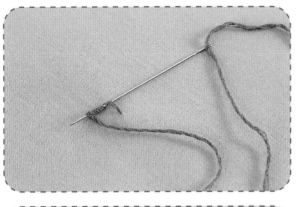
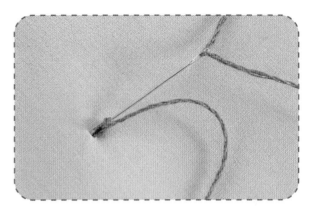

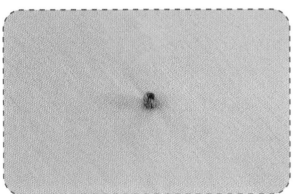
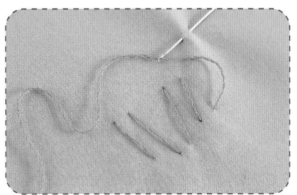

1 Knot the end of your thread then bring it up from the back of the fabric. Wrap the thread around the needle four or five times.

2 Take the needle back through the fabric, just to one side of the start position.

3 Pull the needle through to the back, sliding the knot to the surface of the fabric to complete it. Make a scattering of knots in the same way.

4 To make the stems, create a long stitch by taking the needle in and out of the fabric. Different lengths at angles look natural, but don't make the stitches more than around 4cm (1½in) long as they may catch!

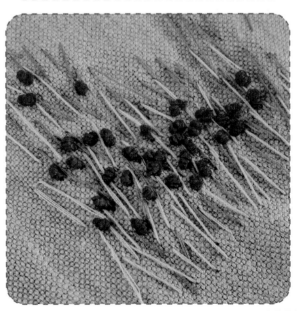

Key techniques

Snipping into curves

Cutting small 'V' shapes into the seam allowance of curves will help to reduce bulk and allow the seam to sit flat without puckering. Pinking shears are useful tools for speedy snipping, or a small, sharp pair of scissors will do the trick!

Cutting corners

To reduce bulk and create sharper points, cut across the seam allowances in the corners of a project that will be turned through, being very careful not to cut through the stitches.

Making a square base

This technique creates a neat, professional-looking bag base. You will complete this stage once you've sewn the base and side seams, with the fabric the wrong way out.

1 Fold the bottom seam over the side seam and pin. Make sure the seams are lined up – you can feel the seams through the fabric.

2 Measure from the point, across the bottom seam as per the instructions, and mark with a pencil. Sew across this line, back-tacking at each end of the stitch line.

3 Cut away the corners of the fabric and turn your bag the right way out to finish.

Applying magnetic clasps

Although they are a simple way to add closures to projects, magnetic clasps don't generally come with instructions, so this may help.

1 Your clasp will be in two halves – one thin and one thick. If applying to a bag with a flap, the thicker part will go on the bag and the thinner one on the flap. Mark the position of the clasp by drawing through the backing disc.

2 Make small cuts either side of the centre spot, either with your quick unpick or a small, sharp pair of scissors. Start small – you can always make a small hole bigger, but if you make the cuts too big you'll just have holes in your fabric!

3 Push the prongs of the clasp through the slits and then the backing disc.

4 Open out the prongs on the back of the fabric. It's a good idea to place a square of fabric behind the clasp to help strengthen the closure, particularly on fine fabrics.

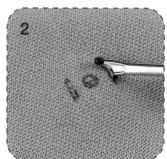
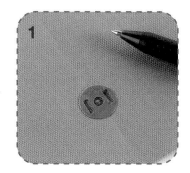
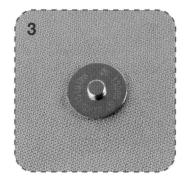
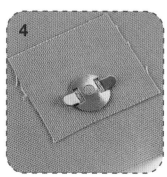

Baby wipe bag, see page 30.

Bias binding

I use quite a lot of bias binding in my projects as it's a simple way to finish off raw edges and it gives a professional finish. Although it can be bought in many colours and widths, I like to make my own as it's not only cost-effective but it also means I can coordinate my fabrics. Bias tape is so called because it is a strip of fabric cut at a 45-degree angle along the bias of the fabric. This allows a little 'give', so that the fabric can stretch around curves without puckering. To cut your fabric accurately you'll need a rotary cutter, rectangular ruler and cutting mat.

MAKING BIAS BINDING

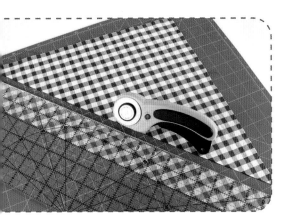

1 Lay your fabric squarely on the cutting mat and, using the 45-degree mark, place the ruler on the straight edge of the fabric. And cut! Use the straight side of the ruler to measure the width you need. For 2.5cm (1in) tape you'll need to cut 5cm (2in) of fabric. As you're cutting the strips, your cut line will become longer, so fold the fabric in half, matching up the diagonal edges, and cut through two, three or four layers at a time.

2 To join the strips together, lay two pieces right sides together, overlapping at right angles. Draw a diagonal line from one corner to the other across the overlap, as shown. Pin, then sew across this line. Trim the raw edge back to around 3mm (⅛in) and press the seam open.

3 Making bias binding involves folding over both the long edges into the centre and pressing. The easiest way to do this is to use a bias tape maker, through which you thread the tape. It folds the strip in two and you press with your iron while pulling the fabric through. If you don't have a tape maker, carefully fold both long edges to the centre of the strip and press. Be careful not to get your fingers too close to the iron!

APPLYING BIAS BINDING

1 To apply the binding, open up the crease lines and, right sides together, pin across the raw edge of your work. Sew with your machine along the upper crease mark.

2 Fold the tape over the raw edge, and use slip stitch (see page 12) to sew by hand. Instead of slip stitching by hand you could machine topstitch.

Tip: continuous bias binding

If you're applying the bias tape continuously, start by opening up the creases and folding over the end of the tape; then pin and machine sew as in step 1, below. When you get back to the start, overlap the ends of the tape by about 5mm (¼in). Fold over and stitch as in step 2, above.

MITRING A CORNER

If the bias binding is attached around a curve it will stretch easily, but if you want to mitre a corner, this is how to do it.

1 Sew along the upper crease line but stop 5mm (¼in) from the corner and back-tack to stop the stitches coming undone. Fold the tape along the second side, making a triangular pleat at the corner. Fold the pleat away from your stitch line and sew straight down the second side.

2 Open up the tape at the corner and you should see a neat mitre forming. As you fold the tape over, mirror the same mitre on the reverse.

3 Secure the back of the tape with slip stitch.

Make-up Remover Pads

Packaged in a pretty box these pads would make a perfect gift! They are made from bamboo towelling, which is incredibly soft, washable and long-lasting. I've used an old cotton T-shirt as a filler, but scraps of the towelling fabric would work just as well.

Finished size

9cm (3½in) in diameter

What you need

Materials for 10 pads:
57 x 46cm (22½ x 18in) bamboo towelling
An old white cotton T-shirt
10cm (4in) circle template

1 Cut out twenty 10cm (4in) circles of towelling and twenty 10cm (4in) circles from T-shirt fabric, using your template.

2 Place two towelling pieces right sides together, then place a T-shirt piece on either side of the sandwich. Sew all around, leaving a turning gap of 2.5cm (1in).

3 Turn right side out.

4 Hand-sew the opening closed to complete. Repeat with the remaining circles.

Tip

To make a natural face
scrub, mix 2 tbsp of raw
honey (or maple syrup
if you're vegan) with 1
tbsp brown sugar. Gently
massage with damp
fingers in circles over your
face and neck, then rinse.
Pat your face with a clean
towelling pad.

Wax Sandwich Wrap

Keep your lunch fresh in these stylish wax wraps. They are so simple to make in your chosen fabric and size. I've used a beeswax bar, but pellets are also available if you prefer. And remember, don't use heat to clean your wraps as the wax will melt – they will easily wipe clean.

Finished size
33 x 33cm (13 x 13in)

What you need
For one wrap:
33cm (13in) square of cotton fabric
Beeswax block (for vegans, soy wax flakes are readily available online)
Jojoba oil
Greaseproof paper
Tea towel
Pinking shears
Iron

1 Cut two pieces of greaseproof paper measuring approximately 38cm (15in) square. Place the fabric over one piece. Grate the beeswax bar over the fabric square – be sparing, as you can always add more wax later. Sprinkle a few drops of jojoba oil over the fabric.

2 Place over the tea towel. Put the second sheet of greaseproof paper over the wax and iron. The wax will quickly melt – use the iron to spread it evenly over the fabric.

3 Allow to cool, then peel away the waxed fabric. Trim the edges with pinking shears.

Variation

Make up wax wraps in different fabrics for each member of the family!

Wax Snack Pouch

This pouch is made using a wax sandwich wrap (see pages 20–21) – simply sew the sides together so your snacks stay put!

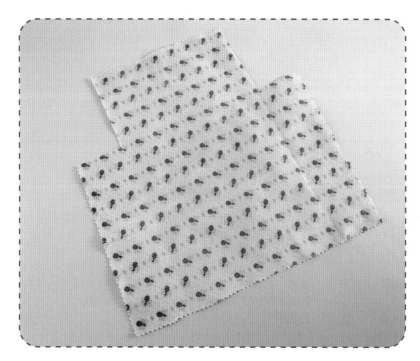

1 Take a 33cm (13in) square wax wrap and cut two rectangles from the top corners measuring 5 x 10cm (2 x 4in).

2 Fold the bottom of the pouch over, right sides together to meet the cut-out sections and sew along each side.

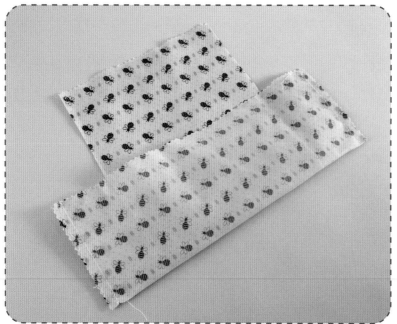

Tip

Use a non-stick or walking foot as you would for a laminated fabric, to help it glide under the needle. Wipe the sewing area clean after you've finished.

3 Turn right side out and push the sewn sides inwards. Now you're ready for snacks!

Bath Sponges

Match the fabric for these pretty bath sponges to your bathroom decor! For the padding inside you could use an old T-shirt, face cloth or any cotton fabric. For mine I've used two layers of bamboo towelling and one of T-shirt fabric.

Finished size

14cm (5½in) in diameter

What you need

For one sponge:

30.5 x 15.25cm (12 x 6in) towelling fabric

15.25 x 15.25cm (6 x 6in) cotton fabric

An old white cotton T-shirt

15.25cm (6in) circle template

18cm (7in) length of 2.5cm (1in) wide elastic

1 Cut one cotton circle, two towelling circles and one T-shirt circle, using your template.

2 Place the elastic on the right side of the cotton circle. Sew the edges of the elastic to the cotton circle, within the seam allowance. Trim off the excess.

3 Place the towelling and T-shirt circles over the elasticated side of the fabric and sew all around, leaving a turning gap of 2.5cm (1in).

4 Turn right side out and hand-sew the opening closed with slipstitch (see page 12).

Tip

To make luxurious bath salts, combine 6 tbsp of sea salt with 3 tbsp of Epsom salts, then add a few drops of your favourite essential oils. Bliss!

Hemp Tote Bag

Hemp is a wonderfully strong, natural fabric that comes in many weights. This bag is made from hemp canvas, which becomes softer over time. To help stop the fabric from twisting, as it's quite a loose weave, I've interfaced the back of each section, but this is optional. I experimented with natural dyes and found that pear leaves create a deep green colour that becomes more lime-coloured when turmeric is added.

1 Boil the handful of leaves in a large pan of water for around half an hour. Add 1 teaspoon of turmeric, a splash of white vinegar and the alum. Dip a small piece of your chosen fabric into the dye to test the colour. I tried both cheesecloth and hemp and achieved quite different colours, as you can see below!

Cheesecloth

Hemp

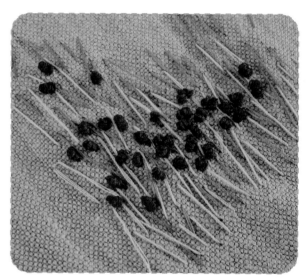

2 Dip the hemp fabric about halfway into the hot pan and hold for a few seconds. Remove and allow to drip dry over the sink or outdoors. Once dry, cut two pieces measuring 38 x 41cm (15 x 16in) for the front and back, two measuring 10 x 41cm (4 x 16in) for the sides and one measuring 38 x 10cm (15 x 4in) for the base. Finish the edges with either an overlocker/serger or the zigzag stitch on your machine to prevent fraying.

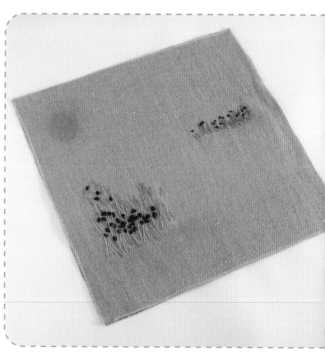

3 With a combination of light and dark green embroidery threads/floss, make a patch of random vertical lines to the left side of the green area to represent grass, then use the darker green only to make smaller stitches on the right side, slightly higher but still on the dyed green section. The smaller stitches and darker green give the illusion of perspective.

4 Make a scattering of large French knots over the larger stitches, using all six strands of thread/floss (see page 13). Sew the knots unevenly across the green stitches for a natural look. Split a length of red thread/floss in half and use three strands to create French knots over the smaller green stitches on the right.

5 Make a weak paste from a teaspoon of turmeric and a drop of water, then use a paintbrush to swirl the mixture in a circle to the top left of the fabric to create a sun, then add a few brushstrokes under the poppies to create shadows. Leave to dry.

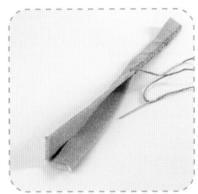

6 Fuse interfacing to the back of each bag panel. This will strengthen the bag but also cover the back of the embroidery stitches to help prevent anything catching on them.

7 Sew the front, back and side panels right sides together.

8 Sew in the base panel, right sides facing, and turn right side out.

9 To make the straps, cut two lengths of hemp fabric measuring 10 x 35.5cm (4 x 14in). Fold the long edges to the centre then fold the whole strip in half and press. Sew over the open edge with jute twine.

10 Repeat with the second handle.

11 Sew over the seams of the bag with twine in the same way, taking a 1cm (½in) seam allowance. Make the stitches approximately 2.5cm (1in) apart, enclosing the raw edges inside the bag. (A little like a reverse French seam.) Fold the top of the bag over by 5mm (¼in) and press, then sew around the top. Hand-sew the handles to each side of the top of the bag, 10cm (4in) in from each side.

Baby Wipe Bag

This double-pocket bag has one pocket for clean wipes and one for used, with a handy pocket in the centre to hold your water spray! I've used cork fabric for the lining as it is antibacterial and water-resistant – this means the wet wipes won't leak and it can be wiped clean.

Finished size

30.5 x 16.5 x 2.5cm
(12 x 6½ x 1in)

What you need

41 x 94.5cm (16 x 37in) cork fabric

69 x 36cm (27 x 14in) outer fabric

94.5 x 36cm (37 x 14in) light fusible fleece

2 30.5cm (12in) zips

1cm (½in) D-ring

Swivel clasp on a ring

Magnetic snap fastener

Clips for pinning

1 To make the flap, cut two pieces of cork, each measuring 30.5 x 18cm (12 x 7in). Fuse fleece to the wrong side of one piece.

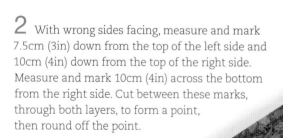

2 With wrong sides facing, measure and mark 7.5cm (3in) down from the top of the left side and 10cm (4in) down from the top of the right side. Measure and mark 10cm (4in) across the bottom from the right side. Cut between these marks, through both layers, to form a point, then round off the point.

30

3 Sew the two flap pieces right sides together, leaving a turning gap of about 7.5cm (3in) in the top seam. Snip off the seam allowances at the corners and trim around the curve.

4 Turn right side out and press, then edge stitch around the seam, leaving the top unsewn.

5 Fit the thinner side of the magnetic snap just above the curved point, just through the un-fleeced side.

6 Cut four pieces of cork fabric and four of fabric measuring 32 x 18cm (12½ x 7in). Fuse fleece to the wrong sides of the fabric pieces.

7 Sew the top of the flap to the right side of one fabric piece, 4cm (1½in) from the top, with the snap facing down.

8 Cut four pieces of fabric measuring 5 x 7.5cm (2 x 3in). Fold the long edges to the centre and press, then fold in half and press again.

9 Slip the ends of the zips inside the folded fabric pieces and sew, then trim the excess fabric to the width of the zips.

10 Take two of the fabric pieces and sew them right sides together, 4cm (1½in) in from each side and the bottom, starting and finishing 2.5cm (1in) from the top. Reverse stitch a few times to make the seam strong.

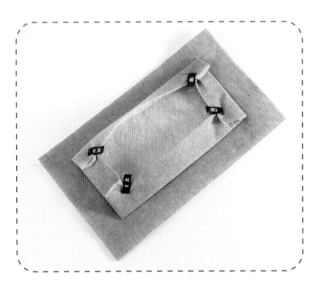 

11 Clip one layer of fabric to the centre, as shown.

12 Sew one of the zips, right sides facing, centrally to the top of the fabric. The zipped section should be 5mm (¼in) shorter than the fabric at each end.

13 Sew a cork piece to the wrong side of the zip, so one edge of the zip is caught between the fabric and the cork pieces.

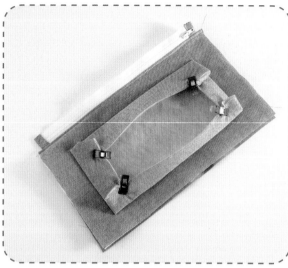

14 Fold the two pieces wrong sides together and edge stitch along the side of the zip.

15 Take the fabric with the flap and sew it to the remaining side of the zip, then sew a cork piece to the back of the zip. Fold over as before and edge stitch along the zip.

16 Open out the clipped fabric. Sew the second zip to the top of this piece, then a cork piece to the back side. Repeat with fabric and cork on the remaining side of the zip.

17 Cut a length of cork measuring 7.5 x 5cm (3 x 2in). Fold the long sides to the centre, then fold the piece in half and press. Sew along both sides. Thread through the D-ring.

18 Sew, facing inwards to one side of the bag, just underneath the flap. Make sure you sew just through the outer fabric, not the cork lining.

19 Clip the whole of the top pocket away from the edges. I prefer to use clips instead of pins so I don't spike myself when I turn the bag right side out!

20 With the zip open, sew the fabric and cork pieces right sides together, cork to cork and outer to outer, leaving a turning gap in the bottom of the cork side of about 10cm (4in). It will feel bulky as you sew around the fabric side so take your time, and make sure you don't trap the flap in the seams. Snip across the corners.

21 Turn right side out.

22 Push the lining inside the bag – don't close the opening just yet as you'll need it later.

23 Clip the pocket you've just sewn to the centre, away from the side seams.

24 Sew the fabric and cork pieces right sides together, outer to outer and cork to cork, leaving a turning gap as before. It will be even more bulky now, so lots of clips may help! Snip off the seam allowances at the corners.

25 Turn right side out and push the lining inside the bag. Close the zips. Fold over the flap and mark the position of the second half of the magnetic snap. Fit the snap over this mark, just through the top layer of fabric. You'll need to put your hand through the turning gap in the lining to do this. Sew the openings in both lining pieces closed. Push the linings inside the bag.

26 To make the wristlet, cut a length of cork measuring 5 x 35.5cm (2 x 14in). Fold the long sides to the centre, then fold in half and press. Thread through the swivel clasp ring.

27 Open the ends and sew right sides together.

28 Re-crease the folds and sew all the way around. Slide the ring over the seam and sew straight across the handle just above the ring. Clip onto your bag.

Inside your bag you'll have two zipped pockets for wet and dry wipes and a handy centre pocket for storing your spray!

Bottle Bag

This sturdy bag will easily carry four bottles back from the supermarket, or more if the bottles are small! The bag is soft enough to fold or roll for easy storage. I've used recycled cloth canvas for my tote, which makes a strong bag that doesn't need lining. Other suitable fabrics are denim or home-decor weights, but recycling old curtains would be ideal!

1 Cut four pieces of fabric measuring 35.5 x 35.5cm (14 x 14in). Fold the top of one piece over to the right side by 5mm (¼in) and press; fold over again by 2.5cm (1in) and press. Slip the lace just under the fold and sew. Fold the whole piece in half and crease, this will help when sewing the bag up later. Repeat for the other three pieces.

2 Cut the webbing in half. Place one piece over one side of the bag 7.5cm (3in) in from each side, with the ends 5mm (¼in) up from the bottom edge. Sew along each side of the strap to secure, stopping just under the lace. Repeat with one more panel.

3 Sew one handled piece wrong sides together with one piece without a handle. Take a 5mm (¼in) seam allowance, leaving the top edge open. Snip across the seam allowances of the bottom corners.

4 Turn inside out. Sew around the seam one more time with a 1cm (½in) seam allowance. The raw edges should be trapped inside the seam. Make sure you sew across the ends of the webbing in the bottom seam.

5 Turn right side out, then repeat with the second two panels.

6 Place the two bags together, with the handled sections on the outside. Sew straight up the centre crease through all layers, stopping just under the lace, as you may find the fabric too thick to sew through at the top.

Stocking Gift Bags

Birthdays, holidays, weddings and anniversaries... just think about how much you'd normally spend on wrapping paper and disposable bags. Then think about making your own packaging that can be re-used year after year! Handmade gift bags are part of the gift, and can either be kept by the recipient and used as storage, or passed on at the next gift-giving event. I've designed a few different shapes and sizes for this book, which can be re-sized if necessary. This cute stocking makes a perfect reusable gift bag for smaller presents and can even hang on the Christmas tree!

Finished size
23 x 18cm (9 x 7in)

What you need
For one stocking:
41 x 23cm (16 x 9in) outer fabric
41 x 23cm (16 x 9in) lining fabric
26.75 x 13cm (10½ x 5in) fabric for the cuff
26.75 x 10cm (10½ x 4in) fabric for the drawstring section
41cm (16in) of 1cm (½in) wide ribbon to draw
25.5cm (10in) of 1cm (½in) wide ribbon to hang
Button or bell (optional)
Stocking template (see page 95)
Safety pin or bodkin

1 Cut out two mirrored outer and two mirrored lining pieces using your stocking template. Sew the outer pair right sides together, leaving the top open. Repeat with the lining fabrics, this time leaving a turning gap in one side of the lining of about 7.5cm (3in). Snip into the seam allowances of the curved seams, then turn the outer stocking right side out.

2 Sew the short ends of the cuff fabric right sides together to make a tube.

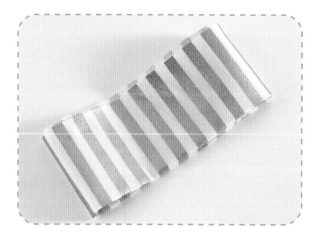

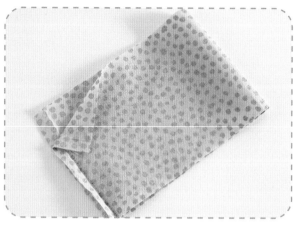

3 Fold the cuff in half, wrong sides together, then press.

4 Take the fabric for the drawstring section and press the short ends to the wrong side by 5mm (¼in). Unfold, then sew the short ends right sides together along the crease, leaving 2.5cm (1in) at the top unsewn.

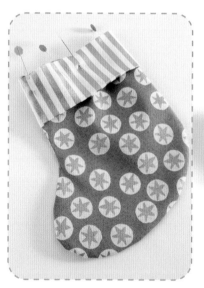

5 Fold the top over by 5mm (¼in) then 1cm (½in) and press. Sew close to the fold to create a channel for the drawstring ribbon.

6 Slip the cuff over the outer stocking, lining up the raw edges at the top, and with the seam placed at the back edge of the stocking. Pin it in place.

7 The drawstring section goes over the top, right sides together with the cuff, with the seam at the back edge of the stocking. Re-pin the top edges.

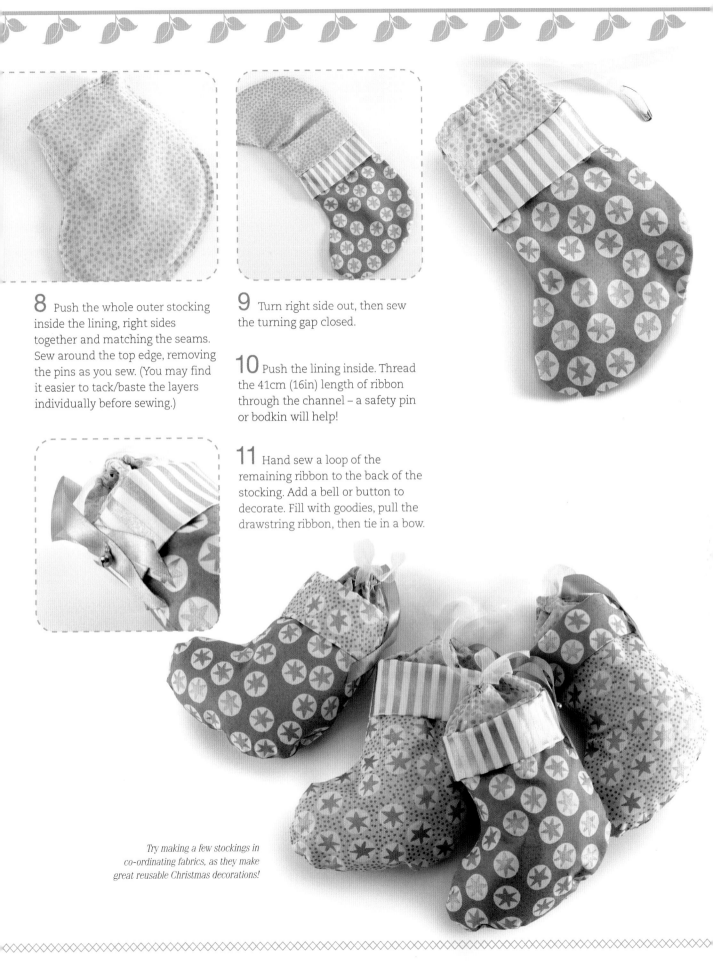

8 Push the whole outer stocking inside the lining, right sides together and matching the seams. Sew around the top edge, removing the pins as you sew. (You may find it easier to tack/baste the layers individually before sewing.)

9 Turn right side out, then sew the turning gap closed.

10 Push the lining inside. Thread the 41cm (16in) length of ribbon through the channel – a safety pin or bodkin will help!

11 Hand sew a loop of the remaining ribbon to the back of the stocking. Add a bell or button to decorate. Fill with goodies, pull the drawstring ribbon, then tie in a bow.

Try making a few stockings in co-ordinating fabrics, as they make great reusable Christmas decorations!

Grocery Bag

My ideal grocery bag is strong, lightweight, washable and not too large... after all, I need to be able to carry it when it's full! This bag is made from recycled bottle fabric with a denim lining and has a wipe-clean, water-resistant cork base. It ticks all the boxes for my shopping trip! Use a 1cm (½in) seam allowance.

Finished size

24 x 29.25 x 16.5cm
(9½ x 11½ x 6½in)

What you need

86.5 x 23cm (34 x 9in) outer top fabric

86.5 x 18cm (34 x 7in) cork fabric

86.5 x 61cm (34 x 24in) lining fabric

86.5 x 41cm (34 x 16in) fusible fleece

1 Cut two pieces of outer top fabric measuring 43.25 x 23cm (17 x 9in), and two of cork fabric measuring 43.25 x 18cm (17 x 7in). Sew the cork right sides together to the bottom of the top fabric. Press the seam away from the cork. Fuse fleece to the wrong side of the bag outer – you won't be able to iron cork from the right side, so use a medium heat to fuse the fleece on the wrong side. Topstitch along the top side of the seams.

2 To make the handles, cut two lengths of lining fabric measuring 10 x 63.5cm (4 x 25in). Fold the long edges to the centre, then fold in half and press. Topstitch along both sides.

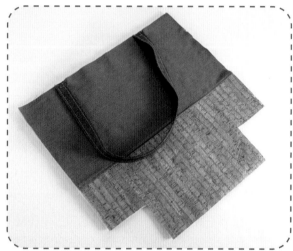

3 Cut a 9cm (3½in) square from each bottom corner of the bag outer pieces. Use one piece as a template to cut two lining pieces. Sew the handles to the top of the outer bag sections, facing inwards, 10cm (4in) in from each side.

4 Sew the top of one lining piece to the top of each outer piece, right sides together.

Variation

This bag is also the perfect size to use for storage. Use a firm interfacing and make the handles shorter to create a handy cube in which to keep anything from craft supplies to toys! And, of course, you can substitute the cork fabric, if you prefer.

5 Sew the two pieces right sides together, outer to outer and lining to lining, matching the seams. Leave the cut-out corners unsewn, and leave a turning gap in the base of the lining of about 13cm (5in). Pinch the cut-out corners so that the side seams sit over the base seam, then sew to make the bag base square (see also page 14).

6 Turn right side out, then sew the opening closed. Push the lining inside the bag, then topstitch around the top edge to finish.

Plant Pot Covers

Plastic plant pots aren't the prettiest of things, but many plants are grown in them. Instead of throwing them away, why not disguise them with fun fabric bowls? You will need to place the pots onto a tray so that the fabric bowls don't get wet – a small plate or the bottom cut off a plastic bottle will do the job.

What you need

The fabric and finished size depends on the size of your pot.

My pots measure 7.5 x 6.5cm (3 x 2½in), and for each one I used a 23cm (9in) square of hessian/burlap. Any natural fabric will work, so use a cotton print if you prefer. I used a length of hessian/burlap string to hold the fabric in place while it dried, and decorated each cover with a 20.5cm (8in) length of lace.

You'll need a container slightly larger than your pot to use as a mould – a ramekin dish was the perfect size for mine!

The fabric stiffener consists of 1 cup (240ml) of water, ½ cup (65g) of plain flour, 1tbsp of sugar and 1tbsp of lemon juice.

1 Mix the fabric stiffener ingredients together in a saucepan and heat the mix on the hob on a low to medium heat until it is the consistency of single cream.

2 Paint the mixture over the fabric square.

3 Drape the fabric over the mould and tie it in place with string. Trim the corners off the fabric to create a more even top edge. Leave to dry upside down.

4 When dry, remove the string and glue a length of lace in its place. Why not make up a trio of plant pot covers to create a unique display?

Variation

Use different-shaped moulds to make small decorative bowls, such as for storing items like eco-friendly cotton buds/swabs.

Fabric Gift Wrap

The Japanese have been using a form of reusable gift wrap, called *furoshiki,* for over a thousand years. You can wrap any size or shape of gift using no paper or sticky tape, and the fabric can then be reused or even worn as a headscarf. Each of my gifts used 1 square metre (1 square yard) of fabric. Either hem by rolling the raw edges over twice and sewing, or use a rolled hem on your overlocker/serger. You may need a larger or smaller square depending on the size of your gift. My plain fabric is calico and the patterned fabric is viscose, but any fabric with a drape will work well.

Wrapping and tying

For these two boxes, place the box diagonally in the centre of the fabric, pull all four corners together tightly around the box. Tie a piece of ribbon or string around the bunched fabric and then push the pointed ends of the fabric into the centre.

Wrapping boxes

1 Place your box diagonally in the centre of your fabric square. Pull two corners tightly around the box and knot.

2 Tie the remaining two corners together in a knot.

3 Decorate with dried or fresh flowers.

Wrapping bottles

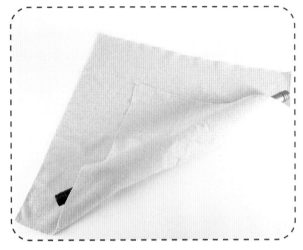

1 Wrapping two bottles is easy – you add protection for the bottles and create a useful carry handle! Place the bottles end to end, 15cm (6in) apart, diagonally across the fabric.

2 Fold one corner of fabric over the bottles.

3 Roll the bottles tightly in the fabric.

4 Pull the ends together and knot.

Gift Cube

Gifts for any occasion can be beautifully presented in these stylish cubes. I've kept them simple, but you could really dress them up with bows, beads and tassels, if you wish!

Finished size

20.5 x 20.5 x 20.5cm (8 x 8 x 8in)

What you need

90 x 46cm (35 x 18in) outer fabric

90 x 46cm (35 x 18in) lining fabric

82 x 43cm (32 x 17in) single-sided fusible foam stabilizer

4 buttons

50cm (20in) of 1cm (½in) wide ribbon

1 Cut four pieces of fusible foam measuring 20.5 x 43cm (8 x 17in); the short ends are your top and bottom. Measure 10cm (4in) up from each bottom corner, then cut from this point to the centre bottom. Measure 15.25cm (6in) down from the top corners of each piece, and cut from here to the centre top. Snip off 5mm (¼in) from the top point. Fuse the pieces to the wrong sides of your outer fabric, then cut out all around leaving a 5mm (¼in) seam allowance.

2 Use one of these pieces as a template to cut four lining pieces.

3 Place two of the outer sections right sides together. Sew along one side and down to the bottom point, stitching close to the edge of the foam.

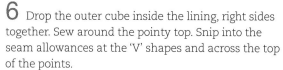

4 Repeat with the two remaining outer pieces, then sew the two sections together. Turn right side out.

5 Sew the lining pieces together in the same way, this time leaving a turning gap in one side of about 7.5cm (3in).

6 Drop the outer cube inside the lining, right sides together. Sew around the pointy top. Snip into the seam allowances at the 'V' shapes and across the top of the points.

7 Turn right side out, then sew the opening closed. Push the lining inside the box and edge stitch around the pointy top seams.

8 Sew the buttons to the inside of each point.

9 Fold the tips of the points over to the outside by 2.5cm (1in) and hand-sew in place. Thread ribbon through each point and pull and tie in a bow to close the cube.

Variation

To make a smaller cube measuring 15 x 15 x 15cm (6 x 6 x 6in), substitute these measurements. Cut four pieces of fusible foam measuring 15 x 34.5cm (6 x 13½in). Measure 7.5cm (3in) up from each bottom corner, cut from this point to the centre bottom. Measure 11.5cm (4½in) down from each top corner, cut from here to the centre top. Snip off 5mm (¼in) from the top point, then continue as for the larger cube.

Gift Bags

Birthdays, weddings, Christmas, anniversaries… there are so many occasions on which we give gifts! These gift bags can be re-used year on year and made in any size you like. They also make useful storage bags!

Finished size for the small bag

29.25 x 21.5 x 6.5cm (11½ x 8½ x 2½in)

What you need

61 x 25.5cm (24 x 10in) bottom (bird) fabric

61 x 10cm (24 x 4in) top (leaf) fabric

61 x 33cm (24 x 13in) lining fabric

127cm (50in) of 1cm (½in) wide ribbon

Cut

2 pieces of bottom (bird) fabric measuring 30.5 x 18cm (12 x 7in)

2 pieces of top (leaf) fabric measuring 30.5 x 10cm (12 x 4in)

2 strips of bottom (bird) fabric measuring 29 x 6.5cm (11½ x 2½in)

2 strips of lining fabric measuring 30.5 x 3.25cm (12 x 1¼in)

2 pieces of lining fabric measuring 30.5 x 29cm (12 x 11½in)

1 Fold the two 30.5 x 3.25cm (12 x 1¼in) lining strips in half lengthways, right sides together, and press.

2 Sew this folded strip to the top of one of the 30.5 x 18cm (12 x 7in) bottom pieces, raw edges meeting. Sew the bottom of one of the top pieces of fabric right sides together to this seam, so the lining strip is sandwiched in between the top and bottom. Repeat for the second side of the bag.

3 Fold the short ends of the 29 x 6.5cm (11½ x 2½in) bottom (bird) strips over to the wrong side by 1cm (½in) and sew.

4 Fold the strips in half lengthways, wrong sides together, then press. Sew one to the centre of the right side of each top piece, raw edges matching, to make the channels for the ribbon ties.

5 Sew the lining pieces to the tops of the outer pieces, right sides together. Check the lining is the same length as the outer, and if not, trim to match.

6 Sew the bag front and back pieces right sides together, outer to outer and lining to lining, matching the seams. Leave a turning gap in the bottom of the lining of about 7.5cm (3in).

7 Pinch each corner so that the side seams sit over the base seams, then sew across the corners, 4cm (1½in) from each point.

8 Cut across the corners to remove the excess fabric. Turn the bag right side out, then sew the opening closed. Push the lining inside the bag.

9 Cut the ribbon in half. Thread one length through the front casing from right to left, then through the back casing from left to right. Repeat for other ribbon, travelling in the opposite direction. Knot the ends. Pull the ribbons to close.

Making a larger version

Follow all of the steps as before, but in step 7, you should sew 5cm (2in) from the points.

Tip

Experiment with sizes: a long slim bag would be perfect for bottles (a bit of wadding/batting will help to protect them), or small bags would be ideal for sweets or jewellery.

Finished size for the large bag

20.5 x 30.5 x 9cm
(8 x 12 x 3½in)

What you need

61 x 30.5cm (24 x 12in) bottom fabric

61 x 15.25cm (24 x 6in) top fabric

61 x 38cm (24 x 15in) lining fabric

127cm (50in) of 1cm (½in) wide ribbon

Cut

2 pieces of 30.5 x 23cm (12 x 9in) bottom fabric

2 pieces of 30.5 x 15.25cm (12 x 6in) top fabric

2 strips of bottom fabric measuring 29.25 x 6.5cm (11½ x 2½in)

2 strips of lining fabric measuring 30.5 x 2.5cm (12 x 1in)

2 pieces of lining fabric measuring 30.5 x 37cm (12 x 14½in)

Repair Kit

One of my Mum's sayings was 'mend, don't spend!', and I still bear this in mind when I find a split or tear in my clothing. Fill this handy case with products to help your wardrobe live longer. Needles and thread for a quick repair on split seams; fusible webbing for the hem that's come down, and safety pins to hold it up until you can get to an iron; a small pair of scissors; and anything else you need! I've added a spot-cleaning kit consisting of a spray bottle filled with white vinegar and a small jar of bicarbonate of soda. Sprinkle soda on the stain, spray with vinegar (this may fizz a little!) then wipe away.

1 If you haven't already, sew the bias strips together. Fold the long edges to the centre and press – you may wish to use a bias tape maker for this (see page 16).

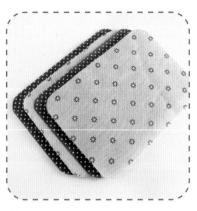

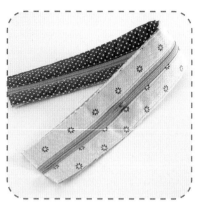

2 Fuse fleece to the wrong sides of each outer fabric piece. Use your 5cm (2in) circle template to round off the corners of the 25.5 x 18cm (10 x 7in) lining and outer kit pieces.

3 Cut the ends off the zip to make it 63.5cm (25in) in length. Sew right sides together to one of the 63.5cm (25in) outer fabric strips.

4 Sew a strip of lining to the back side of the zip, sandwiching the zip tape in between the two pieces. Repeat with the remaining two strips of fabric on the other side of the zip. Press, then topstitch along each side of the zip. Tack/baste along the raw edges within the seam allowance.

5 Sew the 16.5 x 9cm (6½ x 3½in) outer and lining zip ends right sides together to one end of the zip panel. Press, then topstitch along the seam.

6 Sew the other end of the outer zip end to the other end of the zip panel. Roll up the panel so that the ends of the lining pieces meet right sides together and sew.

7 Open out the roll and you'll have a circular zip panel. Topstitch along the seam you've just made.

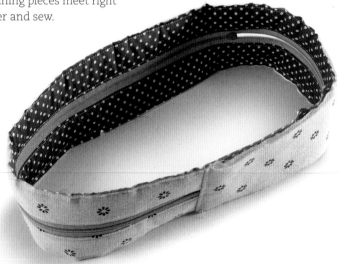

8 Cut the bias binding in half. Sew one piece to the top and one to the bottom of the zip panel, right sides together. Begin by folding the end of the binding over by 1cm (½in), and overlap the ends.

9 Sew the two pocket pieces right sides together along the top edge. Turn right side out and press. Sew 1.5cm (⅝in) from the top to form a channel for the elastic. Thread the elastic through the channel – a safety pin will help!

10 Place the pocket over one of the 25.5 x 18cm (10 x 7in) lining pieces, raw edges meeting. Sew one end of the elastic within the seam allowance. Pull until the elastic is the same length as the fabric and sew, again within the seam allowance. Arrange the gathers evenly. Sew a line down the centre of the pocket to divide it into two.

11 Trim the bottom corners of the pocket to the same shape as the lining, then sew around the raw edges within the seam allowance. Fold the long edges of the handle fabric to the centre, then fold the strip in half. Topstitch along both long sides. Place across the centre of one of the 25.5 x 18cm (10 x 7in) outer pieces and sew each end within the seam allowance. Sew across the ends of the handle again, this time 5cm (2in) from each end (this will create the raised handle). Place the pocketed lining piece wrong sides together to the lid and sew around the edge within the seam allowance.

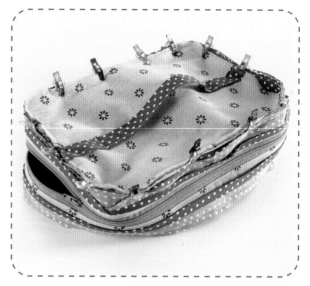

12 Sew the remaining 25.5 x 18cm (10 x 7in) pieces wrong sides together to make the base. Mark the centre of each side of the lid and base by folding them in half and making a small snip into the seams, then fold in half in the opposite direction and repeat.

13 Do the same with the zipped panel, marking the centre of the spine (the zip end panel) and the opposite side, match these two points to fold in half and snip into the seams so that you have marked four quarters. Match the marks of the zipped panel to the marks on the lid, with the lining sides together. Make sure the bottom of the pocket matches the spine of the zipped panel. Use plenty of clips or pins to hold them together! Snip into the seam allowance of the zipped panel around the curved corners.

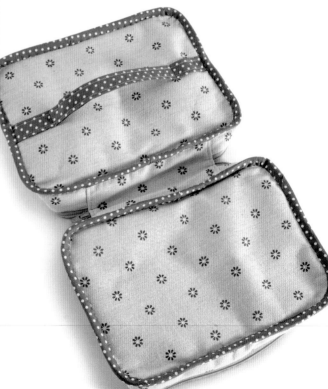

14 Sew all around – you'll find it easier to sew with the zipped panel uppermost. Sew the base in the same way.

15 Fold the bias binding over the raw edges and hand-sew with slip stitch.

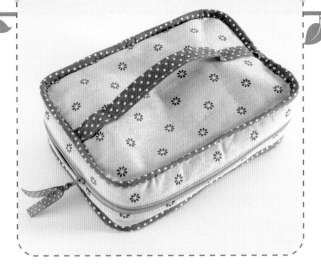

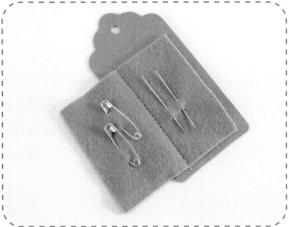

16 Add a 10cm (4in) length of ribbon to the zip pull.

17 Take one of the pieces of card and sew the centre of the felt square to one side of the card. Pop a few safety pins and needles into the felt.

18 Close the felt 'pages' and tie a ribbon around the card.

19 Make small snips into the sides of the remaining card, then use these to secure the ends of a few different coloured threads as you wrap them around the card.

20 Fill your case with care and repair items so you're always prepared!

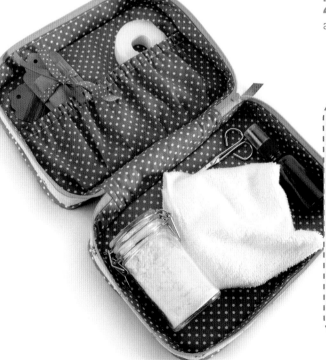

Bowl Covers

Keep insects and dust away from your prepared salads and washed fruit with these simple bowl covers. Be aware that they're not airtight, so won't keep your foods fresher for longer, but they will certainly help keep it clean and add a splash of colour to the kitchen! I've made mine to fit 15.25cm (6in), 20.5cm (8in) and 25.5cm (10in) bowls.

What you need

51 x 56cm (20 x 22in) fabric
267cm (105in) of 2.5cm (1in) wide bias binding
152.5cm (60in) elastic cord
Safety pin or bodkin

1 Cut your fabric into circles measuring 5cm (2in) wider than your bowls. I cut my circles to 20.5cm (8in), 25.5cm (10in) and 30.5cm (12in).

2 Fold the bias binding in half lengthways and press.

3 Slip the binding around the edge of the fabric and sew close to the edge of the binding to create a channel for the elastic. Stop sewing 5cm (2in) before the end, overlap the ends of the binding by 2.5cm (1in), cut the binding and fold the end over by 1cm (½in) before finishing. Repeat with the remaining two circles.

4 Cut the elastic into three lengths measuring 38cm (15in), 51cm (20in) and 63.5cm (25in). Thread the shortest length through the overlap in the binding of the small circle and through the channel. Knot the ends together. Do the same with the medium and large circles.

5 Push the knots inside the bindings to finish.

Apron

I've included an apron in this book because if we keep our clothes clean we'll be using the washing machine less! I've used linen for my apron as it is a strong fabric, easy to clean and thick enough to prevent any dirt going through it onto my clothes.

Finished size

112 x 85cm (44 x 33½in)

What you need

96 x 122cm (38 x 48in) fabric for the apron
102 x 30.5cm (40 x 12in) contrast fabric for the pockets
2 buttons

Cut

1 piece of apron fabric measuring 33 x 89cm (13 x 35in) for the front

2 pieces of apron fabric measuring 40 x 61cm (16 x 24in) for the sides

2 pieces of apron fabric for the straps measuring 11.5 x 63.5cm (4½ x 25in)

1 piece of apron fabric for the facing measuring 30.5 x 10cm (12 x 4in)

4 contrast fabric pieces for the pockets measuring 25.5 x 30.5cm (10 x 12in)

1 To make up the straps, fold each strip in half, right sides together. Sew along the long sides and one short side. Turn right side out and press. Topstitch all the way around.

2 Sew two of the pocket pieces right sides together, leaving a turning gap of about 5cm (2in) in the bottom edge. Snip across the corners, turn right side out and press. Measure 5cm (2in) along from one top corner, fold the opposite corner inwards at this point and press. Repeat for the second pocket, mirror imaging the first.

3 Open out the fold, then topstitch around the corner. Repeat for the other pocket.

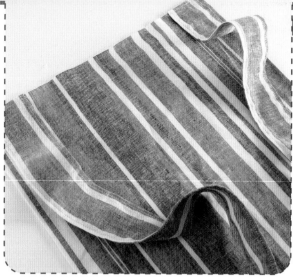

4 Re-fold the corners then sew a button to each point to secure.

5 Take the large front panel, fold the long edges to the wrong side by 5mm (¼in) and press. Sew the raw edges of the straps to the top of the right side of this panel, 5mm (¼in) in from each side.

6 Fold the bottom edge of the facing over to the wrong side twice by 5mm (¼in) and sew to hem.

7 Place right side down over the straps and sew the top edge (the facing should be 5mm/¼in shorter at each end than the apron panel).

8 Turn the facing over to the back of the apron and then edge stitch along the top.

9 Take the two side panels, fold the top of each over twice by 5mm (¼in) and sew.

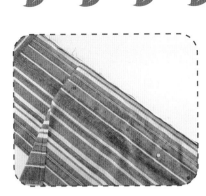

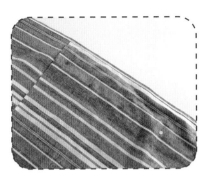

10 Lay the apron front right side down. Right side up, and lining up the bottom edges, push one of the side panels under one of the folds along the sides of the front panel. Pin the pieces in place.

11 Fold the long side edge over by 5mm (¼in) and sew all the way up the side to the top of the bib of the apron.

12 Remove the pins, flatten out the seam and press. Topstitch the seam in place. Repeat for the second side panel.

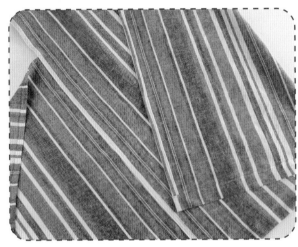

13 Fold the free edges of the side panels over to the wrong sides twice by 5mm (¼in) and sew to hem them. Fold the bottom of the apron over by 5mm (¼in) then 2.5cm (1in) and sew.

14 Pin the pockets over the side seams, 20.5cm (8in) up from the bottom and 16.5cm (6½in) apart. Hold the apron against yourself to check that the pocket position is right for you, then sew around each side apart from the folded section. Remember to back-tack at the start and end to strengthen the seams.

15 Cross the straps, then sew each end to the top corners of the side panels, making sure the straps aren't twisted!

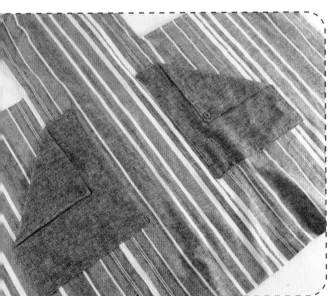

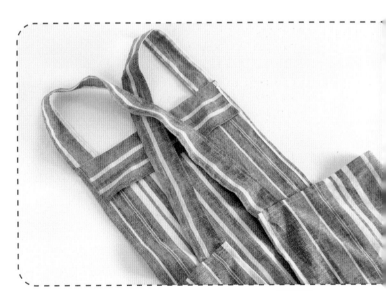

Wipes

We use wipes for so many purposes around the home, from the kitchen to the bathroom. Although these must be the simplest items to make, they can save you a lot of money by replacing the wipes you usually throw away. I've simply cut 30.5cm (12in) squares from bamboo towelling and overlocked/serged the edges. If you don't have an overlocker/serger, use a small zigzag stitch to finish off the raw edges. That's it! Here are a few ideas for using your wipes.

Baby wipes

What you need

Towelling wipes
Pre-boiled water
Organic coconut oil
Spray bottle

Fill your spray bottle with water and add a few drops of coconut oil. Spray and wipe as you need to!

Tip

Always check with your health visitor or doctor before using anything on your baby's sensitive skin.

Tumble drier sheets

What you need

Towelling wipes
White vinegar
Water
Your favourite essential oil
Jar

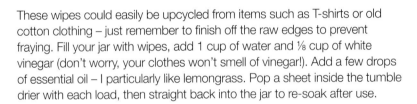

These wipes could easily be upcycled from items such as T-shirts or old cotton clothing – just remember to finish off the raw edges to prevent fraying. Fill your jar with wipes, add 1 cup of water and ⅛ cup of white vinegar (don't worry, your clothes won't smell of vinegar!). Add a few drops of essential oil – I particularly like lemongrass. Pop a sheet inside the tumble drier with each load, then straight back into the jar to re-soak after use.

Kitchen wipes

What you need

Towelling wipes
White vinegar
Lemon peel or chopped lemons
Your favourite scented herb – try rosemary, mint or pine
Jar

Don't throw away old towels or tea towels, as these can easily be upcycled into reusable kitchen wipes. Fill your jar with lemon peel and pour over the vinegar. Add a herb sprig and leave to soak for about a day. Decant into a spray bottle for ease of use if you wish.

Foldaway Bag

You'll always have a shopping bag handy with this slimline foldaway bag. Make up a few and keep them in your handbag and car. I've used a non-directional print, as this makes best use of the width of the fabric.

Finished size

34.5 x 38cm (13½ x 15in)

What you need

81.5 x 63.5cm (32 x 25in) fabric

3 snap fasteners consisting of 1 'male' and 2 'female' parts

Cup or mug as a template

Cut

1 piece of fabric measuring 81.5 x 37cm (32 x 14½in) for the main bag

2 pieces of fabric measuring 13 x 18cm (5 x 7in) for the bag flap

2 pieces of fabric measuring 53.5 x 10cm (21 x 4in) for the handles

1 Fold both short ends of the large piece of fabric over twice by 5mm (¼in) each time and sew to make the hems.

2 Curve the two bottom corners of each piece of flap fabric using a cup or mug.

3 Sew the flap pieces right sides together, leaving the top open. Snip into the curved seam allowances, turn right side out and press. Fit the male snap fastener, centrally, 2.5cm (1in) from the curved hem. Topstitch around the seam.

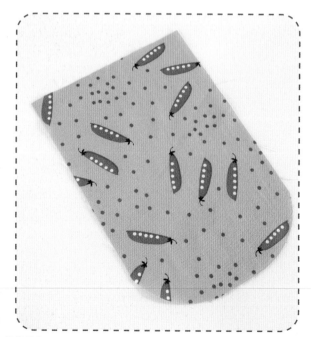

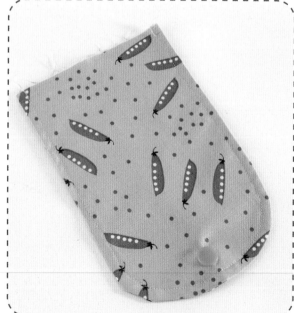

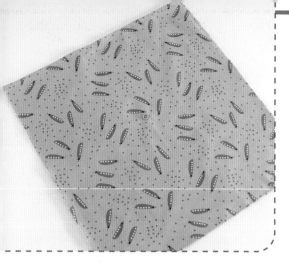

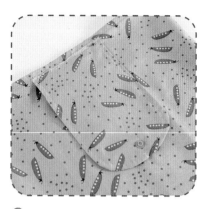

4 Fit one of the remaining snap fasteners to the front of the bag, centrally, 9.5cm (3¾in) down from the top. Fit the last snap fastener to the back of the bag, centrally, 18cm (7in) down from the top. Fold the bag in half, wrong sides together, then sew along each side with a 5mm (¼in) seam allowance.

5 Turn inside out. Re-sew the seams with a 1cm (⅜in) seam allowance, trapping the raw edges inside the seam.

6 Turn right side out. Sew the flap, facing downwards and right sides together, to the centre back of the bag, 2cm (¾in) down from the top. Sew close to the raw edge.

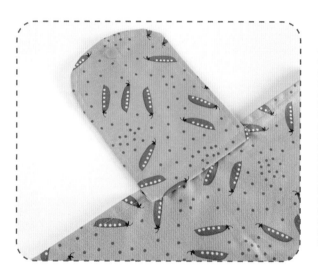

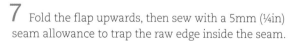

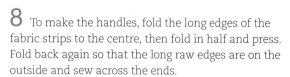

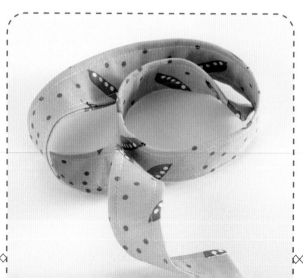

7 Fold the flap upwards, then sew with a 5mm (¼in) seam allowance to trap the raw edge inside the seam.

8 To make the handles, fold the long edges of the fabric strips to the centre, then fold in half and press. Fold back again so that the long raw edges are on the outside and sew across the ends.

9 Turn back again and push out the corners. Edge stitch along the two long sides.

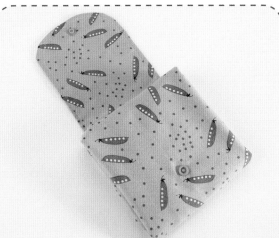

10 Sew the handles to the top of the bag, 9cm (3½in) in from each side. Sew over the ends in a box shape to strengthen the seam.

11 To fold away the bag, open the flap, then fold the sides across the centre. Fold the handles downwards.

12 Fold the bottom of the bag upwards twice.

13 Fold over the flap and close the snap fastener.

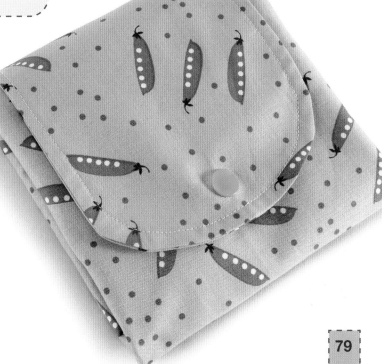

Cork Lunchbag

Take your lunch to work or school in style with this useful, wipe-clean cork-bottomed bag. If you don't want to use it for lunch, this would also make a perfect storage bag for all your sewing notions! Use a 1cm (½in) seam allowance.

Finished size

29.25 x 28 x 14cm (11½ x 11 x 5½in)

What you need

61 x 30.5cm (24 x 12in) cork fabric
61 x 61cm (24 x 24in) lining fabric
66cm (26in) of 1cm (½in) wide ribbon
Toggle lock
Safety pin or bodkin to thread the ribbon

Cut

2 pieces of cork, 30.5cm (12in) square
2 pieces of lining, 30.5cm (12in) square
2 pieces of lining for the drawstring section,
30.5 x 20.5cm (12 x 8in)
2 pieces of lining for the handles, 30.5 x 10cm
(12 x 4in)

1 Cut a 7.5cm (3in) square from the bottom two corners of both the cork and lining bag squares.

2 Sew the cork pieces right sides together along the sides and base, leaving the top edge and cut-out corners unsewn.

3 Pull out the cut-out corners so that the side seams sit over the bottom seam, and sew across to square the base. Flatten the seams to one side as you sew (see also page 14).

4 Repeat for the lining pieces, leaving a turning gap in one side of about 10cm (4in).

Tip

As cork is water-resistant, it makes a perfect, wipe-clean fabric for a bag base. To make the seams waterproof, add a drizzle of wet fabric glue along the stitches.

5 To make the handles, fold the long edges to the centre and press.

6 Fold in half and press. Edge stitch along both sides.

7 Turn the cork bag right side out. Sew the handles, within the seam allowance and facing downwards, to the top of the bag, 7.5cm (3in) in from each side.

8 To make the drawstring section, sew the two pieces right sides together along the shorter sides, starting 4.5cm (1¾in) down from the top. Finish the seams with pinking shears or a zigzag stitch. Press the seams open, then edge stitch around the openings at the top of the fabric.

9 Fold the top over to the wrong side by 5mm (¼in) then again by 1cm (½in). Press, then sew close to the fold to form the channels.

10 Slip the drawstring section over the top of the bag, right sides together and matching the seams. Sew together within the seam allowance.

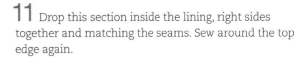

11 Drop this section inside the lining, right sides together and matching the seams. Sew around the top edge again.

12 Turn the bag right side out and sew the turning opening closed.

13 Push the lining and drawstring section inside the bag and press. Sew three times around the top of the bag, in rows 5mm (¼in) apart.

14 Use your safety pin or bodkin to help thread the ribbon through the channels. Thread the ribbon through the channels and add the toggle lock to secure. Enjoy your lunch!

Cutlery Roll

Keep your own cutlery, reusable straw and napkin in your bag and you'll never have to ask for plastic in takeaway shops again! Use a non-directional print for best results. My napkin is a 25.5cm (10in) square of cheesecloth, and I've just overlocked/serged the edges, but an upcycled tea towel would do the trick just as well!

Finished size

7.5 x 25.5cm (3 x 10in), when tied

What you need

62 x 43cm (24 x 17in) patterned fabric

20.5 x 43cm (8 x 17in) plain fabric

20.5 x 43cm (8 x 17in) medium-weight interfacing

46cm (18in) of 1cm (½in) wide ribbon

Cut

1 piece of patterned fabric measuring 20.5 x 43cm (8 x 17in)

1 piece of patterned fabric measuring 20.5 x 35.5cm (8 x 14in) for the back pocket

1 piece of patterned fabric measuring 20.5cm (8in) square for the front pocket

1 piece of plain fabric measuring 20.5 x 43cm (8 x 17in)

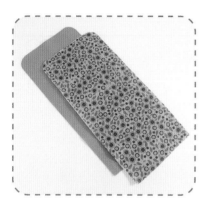

1 Fuse interfacing to the wrong side of the 20.5 x 43cm (8 x 17in) patterned fabric piece. Trim the top corners of both 20.5 x 43cm (8 x 17in) pieces into curves.

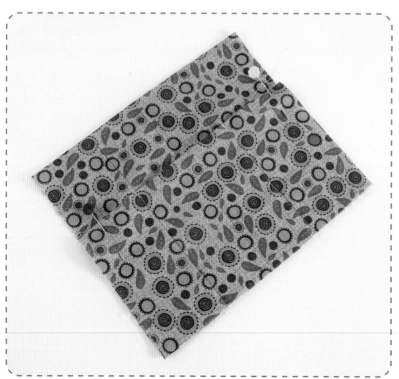

2 Fold the remaining two patterned fabric pieces in half widthways, wrong sides together, and press (they should both measure 20.5cm/8in widthways). Place the smaller piece over the larger, raw edges matching. Measure and mark the centre line, then 5.75cm (2¼in) in from each side. Sew along the 5.75cm (2¼in) lines from the top of the smaller pocket to the bottom. Remember to backstitch a couple of stitches at the top of the pocket to strengthen the seams.

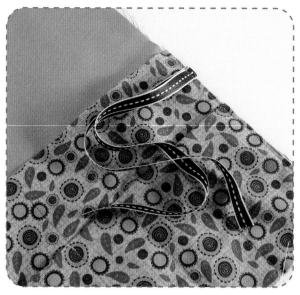

3 Place the pocket panel over the right side of the plain fabric, bottom edges matching. Sew along the centre of the pocket panel through all layers, then along the sides of the pockets within the seam allowance.

4 Fold the ribbon in half and sew the fold of the ribbon, with the ends facing inwards, to one side of the back pocket, 14cm (5½in) up from the bottom edge.

5 Tuck the ribbon inside a pocket, out of the way of the seam. Place the long patterned fabric piece right sides together with the plain and sew all the way around, leaving a turning gap of about 7.5cm (3in) in one side. Snip across the seam allowances at the bottom corners and around the curves.

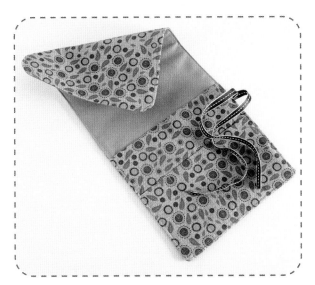

6 Turn right side out and press. Edge stitch all the way around.

7 Place your cutlery, straws and napkin into the pockets.

8 Fold the flap over the cutlery, roll up, and tie the ribbon to secure.

Tip

Cut the ribbon ends at an angle to prevent them from fraying.

Face Coverings

These masks aren't medical grade, but where a face covering is required or preferred it's good to have a few in colours you like, which can be washed and used over again. This style of covering is the simplest to make, with just two rectangles of fabric. You can, of course, make it smaller or larger if you wish.

Finished size

24 x 7.5cm (9½ x 3in)

What you need

51 x 20.5cm (20 x 8in) tightly woven cotton fabric

51 x 20.5cm (20 x 8in) lightweight fusible interfacing

41cm (16in) elastic cord

Simple mask

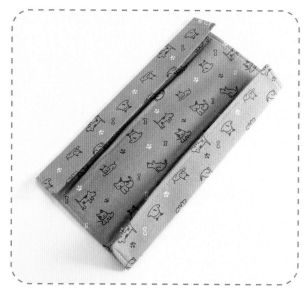

1 Cut two rectangles of fabric measuring 25.5 x 20.5cm (10 x 8in). Fuse interfacing to the wrong side of each piece. Sew the two pieces right sides together, leaving a turning gap in the bottom of about 5cm (2in). Snip across the seam allowances at the corners, turn right side out, then press. Edge stitch all round.

2 Fold the top and bottom edges over by 2.5cm (1in) and press.

3 Cut the elastic in half. Open out the folds in the face covering and tack/baste the ends of the elastic 5mm (¼in) into the folds.

 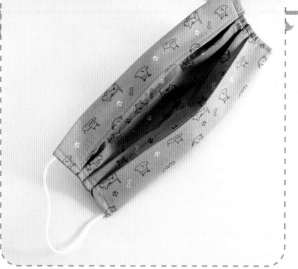

4 Re-fold the top and bottom edges, then make two small pleats across the centre. Pin or clip the pleats in place, then press.

5 Sew along each short end to secure the pleats, backstitching over the elastic to make it secure.

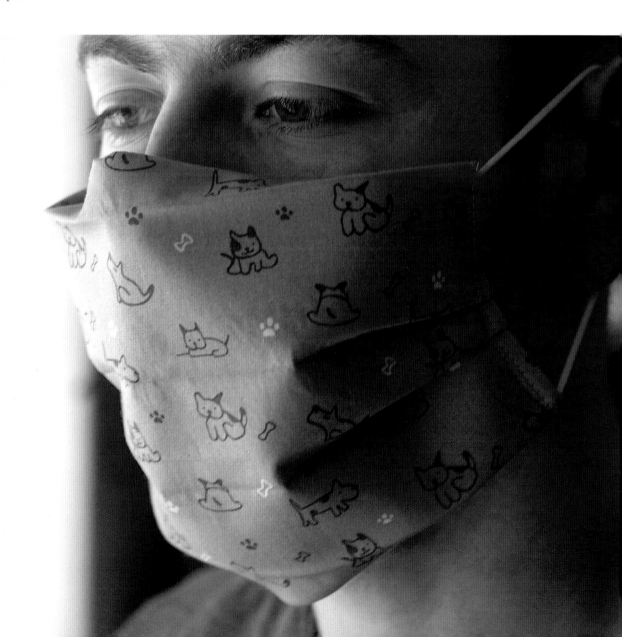

Shaped mask

This mask is slightly more fitted than the face covering on pages 88–89. It is made using a circle of fabric. Make the circle 2.5cm (1in) larger or smaller depending on the size you need.

Finished size

18 x 14cm (7 x 5½in)

What you need

30.5cm (12in) square of fabric

30.5cm (12in) square of lightweight interfacing

51cm (20in) elastic cord

Ruler and marking pen

1 Fold the fabric in half then in half again.

2 Measure 14cm (5½in) from the folded corner in an arc shape, pivoting your ruler in the corner. This will make a 28cm (11in) circle.

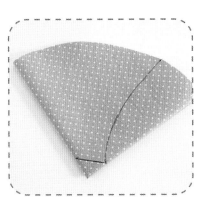

3 Cut out the circle. Measure 2.5cm (1in) along each edge from the folded corner and mark – join the marks together diagonally across the corner. Along the curved edge, measure 5cm (2in) from the double folded corner. Draw a curved line from this point to the right of the bottom diagonal line.

4 Cut along these lines. Open out the two pieces.

5 Sew the pieces right sides together along the curved edge.

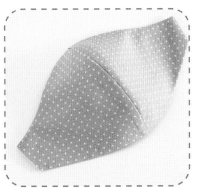

6 Open out the mask so that the raw edges are together, then sew all the way around, leaving one short side unsewn for turning.

7 Turn right side out. Press, turning the open end inwards by 5mm (¼in).

8 Fold the short ends over by 5mm (¼in) to the inside and press. Place the elastic along the fold then sew along the edge to form a channel, being careful not to sew over the elastic!

9 Knot the ends of the elastic together and pull the knots inside the channels to finish.

Mask carry pouch

Keep your face coverings clean and tidy in this simple pouch, which can also be clipped onto a wristlet or lanyard. Keep one in the car and one in your handbag so you're never without a clean mask!

Finished size

21.5 x 15.25cm (8½ x 6in)

What you need

53.5 x 23cm (21 x 9in) patterned fabric

53.5 x 37cm (21 x 14½in) plain fabric

41 x 35.5cm (16 x 14in) fusible fleece

Magnetic snap fastener

1cm (½in) D-ring

2 buttons

1 Cut one piece of patterned and one piece of plain fabric to 39.5 x 23cm (15½ x 9in). Cut one piece of patterned and one piece of plain fabric to 13 x 23cm (5 x 9in). Fuse fleece to the wrong sides of the patterned fabric pieces.

2 Fit the thicker part of the magnetic snap to the large patterned piece, centrally, 18cm (7in) from the right-hand side.

3 Cut two pieces of plain fabric measuring 11.5 x 14cm (4½ x 5½in). Trim the bottom two corners of each into curves. Fuse fleece to the wrong side of one piece.

4 Fit the remaining half of the magnetic snap to the unfleeced side, centrally, 2.5cm (1in) from the curved edge. Sew the two pieces right sides together, leaving the top open. Turn right side out and press, then edge stitch around the seam.

5 Sew the flap, snap facing upwards, to the right (outer) side of the patterned piece, centrally on the left-hand side.

6 Sew the shorter patterned piece right sides together to the left-hand side of the large patterned piece, sandwiching the flap in the seam.

7 Cut a length of plain fabric measuring 7.5 x 5cm (3 x 2in). Fold the long edges to the centre, then fold in half and press. Sew along each side. Thread through the D-ring and fold in half.

8 Sew the tab with the ring facing inwards to the top of the pouch, 1cm (½in) to the right of the seam. Sew the two plain fabric pieces right sides together, leaving a turning gap of about 7.5cm (3in) in the centre.

9 Sew the plain and patterned pieces right sides together, matching the seam. Snip off the seam allowances at the corners, turn right side out and then press. Hand-sew the opening closed.

10 Edge stitch along the two short sides. Fold the two sides towards the centre by 11.5cm (4½in) and press to create two pockets. Edge stitch along the two long sides to hold the pockets in place. Hand-sew the buttons together to the flap. Pop in your masks and close the flap.

Stocking template

The stocking template is given at actual size. Simply trace it off. See pages 40–43.

Index